"Effective Prayer for your Spouse - A Daily Devotional"

By

John Williams

When I was growing up, I do not recall my mom or dad ever praying out loud with me for my future spouse. They had many other things I'm sure that they prayed about. However, with today's divorce rate at approximately 35%, besides the death of a spouse, there is nothing more devastating to a person, family, friends, and community than divorce.

Proverbs 18:22 declares "He who finds a wife finds what is good and receives favor from the Lord.' To find a "Kingdom Husband or Wife" for our children, we will need God's help and guidance. May I also gently add that those who have had a failed marriage(s), I am assuming that you have done the work that you need (Prayer, education, practice, etc.), you're emotionally healthy, and now prepared to be a healthy partner, this book may be of benefit to you. The prayers in this book can also be prayed for your children and future grandchildren.

The prayers contained in this book are scripturally based. Since the creator of marriage is God, it would be best to pray for your spouse based on His word. Regardless of rulings and policies by those who disagree with God's word, and those who will try to reframe marriage in their image, the traditional design by God is clear. The marriage covenant is only between a man and a woman. That said, the content and prayers in this book are unapologetically aligned with Biblical principles and firm in its stance and context.

CONTENTS

Day 1 1
   Pray for A Consistent Daily Devotion and Prayer Time 1
Day 2 2
   Thank God in Advance for His Provision for You Both 2
Day 3 3
   Pray That You Both Will Walk n God's Wisdom 3
Day 4 4
   While Praying for Your Future Spouse, Don't Forget Others 4
Day 5 5
   Pray for God's Strength When You and Your Future 5
Day 6 6
   Pray That You Both Will Trust in The Lord............................ 6
Day 7 7
   Pray That You Both Develop Your Knowledge 7
Day 8 8
   Pray That You Both Will Always Do Your Best...................... 8
Day 9 9
   Pray for A Pliable Heart 9
Day 10 10
   Agree with Your Partner in Prayer...................................... 10
Day 11 11
   When Things in Your Life Are Taking Longer Than Expected 11
Day 12 12
   Have Faith That God Has the Right Person for You............ 12
Day 13 13

Pray for Both Your Destinies 13

Day 14 14
    Pray That You Both Will Listen to Advice and Accept Discipline 14

Day 15 15
    Pray That Your Future Spouse Is Faithful 15

Day 16 17
    Pray for Your Hearts 17

Day 17 18
    Pray That You Both Will Listen...and Well 18

Day 18 19
    Pray for Wisdom in Your Finances 19

Day 19 20
    Keep Feminist Ideology Out of Your Bedroom 20

Day 20 23
    Pray That You Both Will Practice Your Love 23

Day 21 24
    Meditate on Your Identity in Christ 24

Day 22 25
    Pray That You and Your Future Spouse Find 25

Day 23 26
    Worship While You Wait 26

Day 24 27
    Pray Against A Love for The World 27

Day 25 28
    Pray That You and Your Future Spouse Make 28

Day 26 29
    Pray That You Both Will Watch Your Speech 29

Day 27 30

For Men: He Who Finds A Wife Finds A Good Thing	30
Day 28	32
For Women: What Submission Really Means in The Context of Marriage and Why You Should Pray for The Ability to Do It	32
Day 29	35
Pray for A Heart That Submits to Christ	35
Day 30	37
As a License Is to A Doctor to Practice Medicine,	37
Day 31	39
Don't Forget to Have Fun	39
Author's Last Words	40
Author Contact	41

Day 1

Pray for A Consistent Daily Devotion and Prayer Time

In the New Testament, 1 Thessalonians 5:17 (Amp) says: "be unceasing and persistent in prayer."

If we are Christians, our focus should always be to develop our relationship with God, and we should have our own time for daily devotions (Bible reading) and prayers before Him. This centers on us and gives us not only a time to receive from His word (The Bible) and to pray to Him but also an opportunity for God to impart all that He is to us.

Now, concerning a relationship, regardless of whether both partners are knowledgeably prepared for a relationship (If you are not, kindly consider working toward this goal), life will eminently present its challenges. We will also change as we grow individually and together. There will be times when our words may not be clearly understood by our potential partners, no matter our effort or intentions. However, God, through the Holy Spirit, can speak to us and gently convict us of our own mistakes and our contributions to such situations. The result should be the humbling of our hearts, repentance of our sins, the confession of our mistakes and asking for, and rendering forgiveness.

Therefore, we should have our own quiet time. We should pray that our future spouse has or develops a consistent prayer time with the Lord daily. This will also encourage our walk with Him and will develop and grow in us the fruits of the Spirit (Galatians 5:22 & 23). Finally, Jesus said that if we seek the Kingdom of God, and what God wants first, that He would meet our needs as well (Matthew 6:33), kindly say this prayer:

"Dear Heavenly Father, thank you that my future spouse has a genuine love and relationship with you. Give us the zeal to seek your kingdom first and your righteousness. You said that if we do that, you will meet our needs also. Lord, thank you that my future spouse is praying for me daily as I am praying for them. May you develop in us the fruits of the Spirit, according to Galatians 5:22, 23 each day as we walk obediently with you. Thank you, Lord. In Jesus' name, Amen."

Day 2

Thank God in Advance for His Provision for You Both

God has many names. One of my favorites is "Jehovah Roi," proclaimed by Hagar, the servant-maid of Sarah, wife of Abraham. It means the Lord who sees; in some translations: "the Lord God who sees me" or "The Lord who sees to it." She ran away with her son Ishmael and found herself without water and food in the desert. It could have meant certain death for them both. God not only provided but gave her wise counsel as well.

In the context of God's provision for you and your future spouse, I would use two names. 1) "Jehovah Jireh, The One who sees my needs and provides for them." 2) "Jehovah Rohi," The Lord, my shepherd, I shall not want for any good and beneficial thing.

There will be times when it may seem like you may not have all that you need before you meet your partner. Perhaps you already know who they are, but many obstacles stand in the way. Knowing that God is a provider is comforting. Not only is He a great provider, but a loving shepherd as well, and sees the challenges and knows what timing is best. We cannot look into our future, but God can. We can trust that He will always provide the very best for us at the right time and guide and give us wise counsel when we ask. Kindly say this prayer:

"Dear Heavenly Father, I thank you that you see my future spouse and that you know all things. I trust you to provide for us every good and beneficial thing that we need to be together in your perfect timing. I will not fear or worry. Whenever I am in doubt, I will remember to cast my care upon you, for you care affectionately for me (1 Peter 5:7). I thank you for you are my good shepherd and that I can trust you to lead me exactly where I need to go at the right time. Thank you, Lord and I pray this in Jesus' name, Amen."

Day 3

Pray That You Both Will Walk in God's Wisdom

As Christians, we know that the Bible teaches that we are to study to show ourselves approved unto God (2 Tim 2:15). It is through study and prayer that we learn God's wisdom that we may apply it to our lives (Colossians 1:9). Having a future spouse who is wise is profoundly beneficial individually and collectively. Obtaining wisdom will be a lifelong pursuit for both of you, to avoid some of the pitfalls of life.

The book of James is considered the "Proverbs" of the New Testament. James clearly instructs us what to do when we lack wisdom. James 1:5 (NIV) "If any of you lacks wisdom, you should ask God, who gives generously to all without finding fault, and it will be given you." Please say this prayer:

"Dear Lord, I thank you that my future spouse is wise. I pray that they study your word and your ways. Thank you, Lord, for giving them great wisdom as they attain Biblical knowledge. I thank you for leading them in the company of those who are wise. May he/she find a mentor who can give them wise counsel and encouragement. When wise advice is given, I pray that they would hearken to your voice and do what you say. That the voice of a stranger, they will not follow. Thank you, Lord. In Jesus' name, I pray. Amen.

Day 4

While Praying for Your Future Spouse, Don't Forget Others

At the time of writing, I am painfully reminded of a friend who told me that their house, along with four hundred others', were burned to the ground. It was bad enough that she lost the medicine for her disabled child and other critical things in the blaze; she had also lost two nephews, one who was one year old and the other three.

Sometimes we can be so focused on what's going on in our world; we forget that no matter how bad we think we have it, there is always someone who may have it far worse. They may not have a single soul in their lives who knows the Lord and who will pray for them. Would you kindly include others in your prayers during your quiet time today? Listen to needs within conversations throughout your day, that you may identify opportunities to pray for others in need.

Philippians 2:3-5 (NIV) says: "3 Do nothing out of selfish ambition or vain conceit. Rather, in humility value others above yourselves, 4 not looking to your interests but each of you to the interests of the others. 5 In your relationships with one another, have the same mindset as Christ Jesus. Kindly say this prayer:

"Dear Heavenly Father, although I thank you for your many blessings, my future spouse, and the wonderful days that lay ahead. Lord, I want to take this time to lift up: (Pray here for those in need and distress. To be more effective, find the passage(s) of scripture that would apply to their situation). In closing Lord, Jesus said in John 14:12- 14 (NIV) "12) Very truly I tell you, whoever believes in me will do the works I have been doing, and they will do even greater things than these because I am going to the Father. 13) And I will do whatever you ask in my name, so that the father may be glorified in the Son. 14) You may ask me for anything in my name, and I will do it." Thank you, Lord. I believe and receive according to your word. In Jesus' name, Amen."

Day 5

Pray for God's Strength When You and Your Future Spouse Experience Disappointments

We will all experience disappointments in life. When they come, it does not mean that God does not love us. In fact, disappointments and opposition may come when we are faithfully doing precisely what God has told us to do. 2 Corinthians 9:8 (NIV) states "And God is able to bless you abundantly, so that in all things at all times, having all that you need, you will abound in every good work." When tough times come for ourselves and our future spouse, we can pray for God's intervention that we may be able to keep going and prevail. Kindly say this prayer:

"Dear Lord in Heaven, I pray for my future spouse, and I come against the disappointments they maybe facing right now in their lives. Come alongside them Lord and give them the help and support that they need. May you, our great God, frustrate the plans of those who would attempt to do them harm according to 2 Corinthians 9:8. Thank you, Lord, for hearing this prayer in the name of Jesus I pray, Amen."

Day 6
Pray That You Both Will Trust in The Lord

We all have expectations when we believe God for something. But when they take longer than expected, and we grow tired and weary of waiting, what should we do? Is that a time for us to take things into our own hands? Is that a time to make your own plans?

Proverbs 3:5-8 (NIV) says 5 Trust in the Lord with all your heart and lean not to your own understanding; 6 In all your ways submit to him, and he will make your paths straight. 7 Do not be wise in your own eyes; fear the Lord and shun evil. 8 This will bring health to your body and nourishment to your bones.

Some of the most challenging times we face are the thoughts we may have just before we're about to go to sleep. As you think of your day and future spouse, consider doing what is said in the following scriptures. 1 Peter 5:7 (AMP) casting all your cares [all your anxieties, all your worries, and all your concerns, once and for all] on Him. For he cares about you [with the deepest affection, and watches over you very carefully]. Cast your burden on the Lord [release it], and He will sustain and uphold you; He will never allow the righteous to be shaken (slip, fall, fail). Kindly say this prayer:

"Dear Heavenly Father, as my future spouse and I wait for your plan to come to pass, help us to trust you and not do our own thing or go our own way. You can see further than we can, and I trust that you are making all things to work together for our good (Rom 8:28). I pray that the Spirit will help us both to trust you and not lean on our own understanding. Help us to remember to acknowledge you in all our ways, and You promised to direct us. As I lay down to sleep this evening, remind me to cast my cares upon you for you care affectionately for me (Take the time now to tell God about everything that you are concerned about and thank Him for taking care of it). Thank you, Lord, for hearing this prayer for I say it in the name of Jesus, Amen."

Day 7

Pray That You Both Develop Your Knowledge
And Commitment of Your Respective Marital Roles

Currently, where the lies of feminism have crept into Western society and the world, we must not allow this narrative to redefine Godly roles of a man and woman in the context of marriage. As Christians, both men and women have clearly defined roles for a reason, and they are NOT equal. In fact, they are uniquely designed by God, so your marriage and household will produce what He originally intended, and that is Godly offspring (Malachi 2:15).

We obtain this wisdom and knowledge the way we acquire any wisdom and knowledge. We ask God, and we study for ourselves, or we are taught. Proverbs 4:5-7 (NIV) says "5 Get wisdom, get understanding; do not forget my words or turn away from them. 6 Do not forsake wisdom, and she will protect you; love her, and she will watch over you. 7 The beginning of wisdom is this: Get wisdom. Though it cost all you have, get understanding.

Although the Bible is clear on the roles and responsibilities of husband and wife: (Proverbs 31, Eph 5:21-33, Col 3:18-21, Titus 2:1-5 and 1 Peter 3:1-7), many contemporary books go into more specific detail which I found very helpful as well. I have read books like: "Love & Respect," "The Five Love Languages," "For Men/Women Only." and "When Sorry is Not Enough." I have named a few to get you started. However, there are many other books by these and other Christian authors that are insightful, even life-changing. You will find that the knowledge you will gain will be evident when you least expect it and will serve you both for a lifetime. Please say this prayer:

"Dear Heavenly Father, thank you for instilling in me and my future spouse, the zeal to learn the wisdom of your word. Thank you for guiding us to other great resources that will develop our knowledge and commitment to mastering our respective Godly roles as we prepare ourselves to become husband and wife in Christ Jesus. I thank and praise you in Jesus' name, Amen."

Day 8
Pray That You Both Will Always Do Your Best

As Christians, we are called to live to a different standard than those who are not. Romans 12:1 & 2 (NIV) says: 1 Therefore, I urge you, brothers and sisters, in view of God's mercy, to offer your bodies as a living sacrifice, holy and pleasing to God this is your true and proper worship. 2 Do not conform to the pattern of this world, but be transformed by the renewing of your mind. Then you will be able to test and approve what God's will is, his good pleasing and perfect will. The statement: "renewing of your mind" is referring to studying and learning what God instructs us to do in His word; the Bible. The Bible should be our new standard for the way we now live our lives.

The Apostle Paul addresses several issues concerning the Christian family. In the context of this particular passage, what I find interesting is that what he says in the passage, still aptly applies to all. Colossians 3:23 & 24 (NIV) "Whatever you do, work at it with all your heart, as working for the Lord, not for human masters, since you know that you will receive an inheritance from the Lord as a reward."

If I do anything for my spouse and anyone with all my heart, God will see and apply my conduct to my account in Heaven. Although our reward in Heaven should not be the focus, nonetheless, the Apostle Paul declares it as a benefit to all believers. Kindly say this prayer.

"Dear Lord, no matter the circumstances or situations that I or my future spouse face, please help us to do our best in all things according to Colossians 3. We seek to do your will and know that in doing so, our reward, blessings, promotions, and inheritance comes from you. Thank you, Lord. In Jesus' name, Amen."

Day 9
Pray for A Pliable Heart

The Apostle Paul was formerly a persecutor of the faith and a zealot that attacked Christians, Acts 9:1-20. After being spoken to by Jesus our Lord, and regaining his sight, he gave his heart entirely unto the Lord and entered His service. Paul's experience will not be ours, but like Paul, a life fully surrendered to God is one that God can use.

James 5:16 (KJV) says: "Confess your faults one to another, and pray one for another, that ye may be healed. The effectual fervent prayer of a righteous man availeth much." Praying for your future spouse is a stellar habit to develop. It will be something that you both will need to do for the rest of your lives. Having a spouse that has a pliable heart before God will certainly be one that will be pliable towards you. Knowing that God can touch your hearts after a heated disagreement is important for you both. To that end, kindly say this prayer:

"Thank you, Lord, for my future spouse. I thank you that You will help develop in us, hearts that are pliable towards you. May forgiveness for one another flow freely when we disagree, even hurt one another. May we always be willing to be obedient to your direction and to continue to deliberately walk in your ways. In Jesus' name, Amen."

Day 10

Agree with Your Partner in Prayer

Being in agreement, especially in a relationship, is vitally important. The Bible declares this as well in Amos 3:3 (KJV) "Can two walk together, except they be agreed?" Jesus also made it clear concerning the importance of having two people pray together as well. In Matt 18:19 (KJV) "Again I say unto you, That if two of you shall agree on earth as touching anything that they shall ask, it shall be done for them of my Father which is in heaven."

Seeing how you two will be walking through your lives together anyway, it would be good practice to start praying together now, if you know who your future spouse will be. Pray together about everything that is on your minds. Ask each other what you can pray for concerning each other. Perhaps there may be a family member who is sick, pray for them together.

If your future spouse is still on the way, perhaps you can ask a family member, friend, or even your prayer group to agree with you concerning your future spouse. Take this time now to write down what concerns you most at this time and use this powerful principle.

Day 11

When Things in Your Life Are Taking Longer Than Expected

We always face a period in our lives when our circumstances seem to be taking longer than expected. When we get weary, we tend to want to complain and even give up. But know that when things seem to feel most difficult, that is precisely when you're getting closer to your victory. It can be compared to a woman in labor. Her greatest pain comes as she's about to give birth. May I encourage you not to give up? Please don't lose hope. God will come through just as He did before. Stay in faith for your answer or breakthrough. Remember, your breakthrough may not be just for your benefit, but for others as well. When it comes, it will be to God's glory. Hang in there; you can do it.

In the book of Philippians 4:13 (KJV) it says "I can do all things through Christ which strengtheneth me." When you feel like giving up, turn your attention to God. Tell Him, frankly, how you are feeling and ask Him for his strength. Some challenges that come our way are meant for us to learn that we can turn to God and receive His strength. It may seem difficult right now, but don't settle for less. Don't compromise God's best for you.

Finally, in the book of Isaiah 40:31(KJV), it says: "but they that wait upon the Lord will renew their strength. They shall mount up with wings as eagles; they shall run and not grow weary, they shall walk and not faint." If you or your future spouse is weary today, please say this prayer.

"Dear Heavenly Father, I pray that you would help me and (future spouse) today. I am growing impatient, and I am feeling a little tired and weary. Your word declares that we can do all things through Christ, which gives us strength. Lord, I pray for that strength for me and/or for (future spouse), that we may continue and receive your reward and promise to cause all things to work together for our good (Romans 8:28). Finally, help us to wait upon you, Lord, that our strength will be renewed. You promised that if we do that, we will be able to run and not be weary, that we will walk and not faint. Thank you, Lord, in advance for I pray this in Jesus' name, Amen.

Day 12

Have Faith That God Has the Right Person for You

God says that our days were ordained and that our destinies were written in the books of Heaven before we were born. He further declares that his thoughts of us are greater in number than the sands, Psalm 139:16-18. That said, how much more is he concerned about helping you find your future spouse? Don't rush ahead because a wrong spouse can temporarily derail your life.

We can trust that God always has our best interests in mind. We can trust him with our lives down to every detail, especially in finding our Kingdom spouse who will join us for the rest of our lives. Kindly say this prayer:

"Dear Heavenly Father, I know that you love me, and you will cause all things to work together for my good because I love you and I am called according to your purpose (Romans 8:28). You are also able to bless me abundantly, so that in all things always, I will have all that I need to abound in every good work (2 Corinth 9:8 & 9). Father, you also said that if I delight myself in You, that you would give me the desires of my heart (Psalm 37:4).

So, Father, I thank you for arranging a meeting with my future spouse. I will patiently wait for you, knowing that you will always give me your very best. Thank you, Lord. I pray in Jesus' name, Amen."

Day 13

Pray for Both Your Destinies

God has a purpose for each of us. His plan for our lives is recorded in your book in Heaven. Yes, you have a book, just for you, that is maintained in Heaven's library with each of your days recorded. Psalm 139:14-16 (NIV) says, "Your eyes saw my unformed body; all the days ordained for me were written in your book before one of them came to be."

Seeking God to discover your lifelong destiny on Earth is the best and the only way to find out what it is. Praying for yourself and your potential spouse is a way to help you both pursue your purpose individually and together. The best spouse is one who also understands their marriage is meant to complete God's purpose. Please say this prayer:

"Dear Heavenly Father, I thank you because my future spouse and I are fearfully and wonderfully made. I also thank you for your plan and purpose for us on Earth. Father, I ask that you continually reveal to us what your plan for us and our destiny is. May we fully embrace it and support each other as we walk out of our lives pregnant with purpose together for you in Jesus' name, Amen."

Day 14

Pray That You Both Will Listen to Advice and Accept Discipline

Despite what we might think of ourselves, many of us do not like to receive advice and especially, discipline. If we are completely honest, we know that we need both. We need guidance from our parents, Pastor, trusted friends, those in leadership, our employer and finally, our spouse. Good advice can save us from lots of trouble, wasted time and resources. As adults, if we do not heed God's chastisement for the issues in our lives that need to be dealt with, ultimately, He will discipline us. As stern as this sounds, know that He does it not only as the all-knowing God, creator of all things that He is, but also as a loving Father, Proverbs 3:11 & 12). Proverbs 19:20 (NIV) says "Listen to advice and accept discipline, and at the end, you will be counted among the wise." Listening to anyone always takes a certain amount of humility. Let us humble ourselves as God's children that we may listen to sound advice that will ultimately help us to avoid discipline. Please say this prayer:

Dear Heavenly Father, help my future spouse and me to humble ourselves according to 1 Peter 5:6 and anoint our ears to hear sound advice. Help us to be slow to speak and quick to listen James 1:19. We do not and cannot know everything, but we can trust you to bring across our path, those that will provide sound advice and counsel according to Proverbs 11:14. If ever a day comes that we may rebel and not heed your chastisement, I pray that we will humbly repent and receive your discipline to correct us as a Father would to a son and daughter that he loves. In Jesus' name, Amen.

Day 15

Pray That Your Future Spouse Is Faithful

The dictionary defines faithfulness as: "1) strict or thorough in the performance of duty, 2) true to one's word, promises, vows, 3) steady in allegiance or affection.

Today, it is painfully apparent that many in our society do not value faithfulness. We see more people discussing getting a divorce rather than ways to repair and maintain their marriages. We see it in some of the media's attempts to sway the opinions of the masses, instead of staying faithful to the tenets of journalism and report the facts. We also see those in our government who made oaths to serve the people and to obey the law, instead break those oaths and regulations based on their own ideology.

Proverbs 20:6 (NIV) says: "Many claims to have unfailing love, but a faithful person who can find?" When you stand at the altar and pledge your love and faithfulness to your spouse on your wedding day, that should not be the first time. In fact, it should have been evident long before the engagement.

If you do not know who your spouse is, you can pray that they continue to grow and practise faithfulness in their family, church, school, and associations.

If you are in a relationship with our Lord and Savior Jesus Christ, then you know faithfulness is one of the fruits of the Spirit. Galatians 5:22 & 23 (NIV) says: "22 But the fruit of the Spirit is love, joy, peace, forbearance, kindness, goodness, faithfulness, 23 gentleness, and self-control. Against such things, there is no law." All of the fruits of the Spirit are significant, but due to the number of relationships that I have personally seen falter and fail, I felt it worth mentioning. Kindly say this prayer:

"Dear Father in Heaven, I pray that you would build in me and my future spouse a faithful heart. May he/she be faithful first to you and themselves. Bolster them, Lord, when faced with compromise or fear to do what is right. Give them the courage to keep the faith when things get tough. Help us each day to continue to develop a steadfast faithfulness like yours and to walk in the other fruits of the Spirit. In Jesus' name, Amen."

Day 16
Pray for Your Hearts

There are many references in the Bible pertaining to the heart. It discusses the need to guard your heart in Proverbs 4:23 (NIV). The Bible declares that a person with a wise heart, speaks what is right in Proverbs 23:15 & 16 (NIV). It also warns you not to let your heart envy sinners and to be zealous for the fear of the Lord, Proverbs 23:17 & 18 (NIV).

If you already know who your future spouse is, you may be entirely focused on when you see them, and what a wonderful time you will have. It may even consume your thoughts. God knows you're excited to start your new life. But remember that it is He, who will ultimately bring you both together, can help to keep you together.

Matthew says it this way in Matt 6:21 (NIV) "For where your treasure is, there your heart will be also." There will always be opportunities to distract us from our walk and focus on God, even legitimate ones. Make sure, in all seasons and circumstances, that we know what our real treasure is. Kindly say this prayer:

"Dear Heavenly Father, I pray for my heart and that of my future spouse. Lord, develop in us a clean and wise heart that will love you and will speak what is right. Help us to be thankful and grateful for what we have and not be envious of those who have great wealth and things that give the impression of prosperity. Help us to guard our hearts and not lust after things that will entice us away from your plan for our lives. Give us the zeal to reverence you, and lead us in such a way that we gladly treasure you and your ways in our hearts. Father, I thank you for answering this prayer for I pray it in Jesus' name, Amen."

Day 17

Pray That You Both Will Listen...and Well

In almost every book you will find on marriage and relationships, communication is the one thing that is always discussed. The most critical part of that is listening. James 1:19 (NIV) says "My dear brothers and sisters, take note of this: Everyone should be quick to listen, slow to speak and slow to become angry." To be more specific, there are different kinds of listening. There is the kind where we are distracted and hear what is being said, but we're not actually giving our full attention to the speaker. Then, there is listening to form a rebuttal or reply to the speaker. The kind I am talking about is what is called "active" listening.

It takes a certain amount of humility to truly listen to another person. Active listening is where you make yourself a blank piece of paper that the speaker can write on, uninterrupted. You might ask a quick question to validate what is being said, but you are focusing your attention on the speaker in a deliberate effort to understand. You verify by repeating what was conveyed in your own words, i.e., "So if I understand you correctly, you said..." Doing this makes the speaker feel heard, and their words appreciated. If you did it right, they acknowledge that you received their words and heard them correctly. This is the kind of communication that all couples sorely need. Will you try this type of listening? Will you try it today on your future spouse, family, friends or a co-worker? Kindly say this prayer:

"Dear Heavenly Father, I pray that you help my future spouse and me to be the kind of partners that are humble enough to listen to each other. Help us to learn and master the skill of listening that we may better understand and abundantly grow together. Anoint our ears to hear each other, the voice of the Holy Spirit as he guides us into all truth (John 16:13) and our hearts to receive. In Jesus' name, I pray. Amen."

Day 18

Pray for Wisdom in Your Finances

The two things at the top of the list most likely to cause trouble in a marriage are communication and the second, financial troubles. If you are like most couples, one of you might be prone to spend, the other likely to save. Whatever the case, we need to manage and plan our financial resources well. Proverbs 27:23 & 24 (NKJV) says: "Be diligent to know the state of your flocks, and attend to your herds; For riches are not forever, Nor does a crown endure to all generations." In verses, 25 to 27 further states the result of both. In those days where they were mostly an agrarian society (agriculture, farming), today it would equate to our business, occupation, bank, stocks, retirement and investment accounts. The principle remains the same. Know what you have and manage it well as stewards of the blessings our loving God gives to us.

Finally, remember that emotional purchases are almost always a bad idea. I tend to do the following for purchases of $300 dollars or more, if you feel very emotional about a purchase, delay the purchase for 24 hours and pray about it. If you have peace, then make the purchase. If you do not, wait for it. Kindly say this prayer for you and your future spouse:

"Dear Heavenly Father, I thank you for keeping your covenant with us by giving my future spouse and I the ability to obtain wealth (Deut 8:18). Give us a glad heart that will honor you, Lord, with our tithes (Malachi 3:10) from our increase, and give what we purpose in our hearts, not grudgingly or of necessity, for you love a cheerful giver (2 Corinth 9:6 & 7). We thank you for the knowledge and wisdom to manage our finances well individually and collectively. We ask you for witty ideas, inventions and blueprints (Prov. 8:12) that we may bring to fruition for the funding of your kingdom, a legacy for our family. I give you all the thanks and praise in Jesus' name, Amen."

Day 19
Keep Feminist Ideology Out of Your Bedroom
The Authority of Your Bodies Will Belong to Each Other

The focus of this section is to prepare the women's perspective concerning the bedroom for their future husbands. The information is beneficial for men also, and there is a prayer at the end for the men too.

If you do not live in the United States and Europe, this may not apply to you. In Western society, feminism has crept into nearly everything, specifically the schools, government, courts, HR Departments and unfortunately in the minds of children that are now growing into adult women and men. As a son and daughter of God, the moment you invite this false ideology into your heart and soul, it will eventually destroy your marriage. This has especially devastating effects in the marriage bed. Feminist ideology teaches women that their body is their own, and they get to decide what to do with it. This even includes the murdering of an innocent baby.

In fact, when you stand at the altar and say your wedding vows before God and man, a covenant exchange happens. One of the things that happen is the blessing of God's favor comes upon your husband. There is a marriage blessing pronounced over the couple. There is also an exchange of the authority of your bodies. The authority of your body now belongs to your husband, and the authority of his body belongs to you (1 Corinthians 7:2-6). The Apostle Paul says this as a concession (yielding to) not as a command. However, the intent that you are a steward of your body for your spouse is clear. I should also mention, as stewards of your body, you should do your best to keep it healthy and fit for your spouse. Don't make excuses or come up with reasons why you shouldn't. This is also your ministry to your spouse.

Women in the West have also been misguided by TV, films, feminist biased magazines, and internet articles that it is okay to withhold your body from your husband as a punishment if they choose. Many women have done this and unbeknownst to them, at their peril. The wisdom of scripture also teaches a spiritual principle as well. Don't mix worldly advice with God's word. In fact, women are to make themselves available to their husbands as much as it's your ministry to him as his wife. Husbands are to do the same to their wives, showing her the love and care that our Lord continually ministers to His Church (Ephesians 5:22-33). Know that within the context of marriage, each of you is the only outlet for each other when it comes to intimate relations. Never withhold, deprive, or use this gift of God divisively toward each other.

I Corinthians 10:24 (NKJV) shares sound advice which says: "Let no one seek his own, but each one the other's well-being." Deception is one of the greatest weapons that Satan uses in marriage to erode and eventually destroy them. If you are tempted in any way to withhold sex from your spouse, even in just, quickly repent and ask for God's forgiveness. Change your heart, mind and actions to maintain a long and healthy marriage. Never deliberately initiate negative spiritual consequences in your marriage by withholding yourself from your spouse. Doing so may invite harmful vices into your marriage like unwanted masturbation, even adultery. In as much as it is dependent on you, always sow good seed.

In closing, Galatians 6:7 (NKJV) says: "Do not be deceived, God is not mocked; for whatever a man sows, that he will also reap. The Amplified Bible says it this way: "Do not be deceived, God is not mocked [He will not allow Himself to be ridiculed, nor treated with contempt nor allow His precepts to be scornfully set aside]; for whatever a man sows, this and this only is what he will reap." Sincerely say this prayer:

"Dear Heavenly Father, I pray for a humble heart to hear your voice and embrace your word concerning the yielding of my body to my future husband in marriage. Help me to be mindful and steadfast in your precepts. Lord, help me to shun any ideologies, personal preferences, or base teachings etc. that would rail against your word and misguide me from your direction concerning the yielding of my body in the context of marriage. I will meditate when my heart is challenged and will cast down imaginations and every high thing that exalts itself against the knowledge of God (2 Corinthians 10:5).

I will be a doer of your word according to James 1:22 and choose to minister to my husband with my body liberally. Help me to maintain my body through fitness and diet in a healthy way. I commit to keeping the ideology of the world out of our bedroom and loving my dear future husband in the ways that he needs me. In Jesus' name, Amen."

For Men: "Dear Heavenly Father, help me to Love my wife with understanding, tenderness, and care (1 Peter 3:7). Help me to minister to her and love her so my bride will always feel cherished and respected by me. May I serve her emotionally, spiritually and physically with the posture like Jesus, who took off His robe, put on a towel like a servant, and humbly washed His disciple's feet (John 13:4-17).

Help me to stay motivated to keep myself fit and healthy for her through diet and exercise. May I never give her reason to hesitate to give herself to me as a result of my misbehavior. When I do make mistakes, help me to repent, ask her forgiveness wholly and quickly. Remind me to make amends for my offense toward her. May the Holy Spirit heal whatever wounds I may have caused and be the balm that restores her soul. I humbly pray in Jesus' name, Amen."

Day 20

Pray That You Both Will Practice Your Love And Keep It Alive

There is a wonderful book called: "The Art of Loving" by Erich Fromm. The author submits that learning to love someone is tantamount to learning the arts like becoming a classical pianist or prima ballerina. Many students start at a very young age. They practice the fundamentals for many years to be proficient. To reach the highest levels of their art requires continued instruction, practice and discipline.

God shows us that love is a verb; it is something that we do. He planned this from the beginning of creation. **John 3:16 (NIV)** says: "For God so loved the world that He *gave* His one and only son, that whosoever believes in Him shall not perish but have eternal life."

Paul defines it further in **1 Corinthians 13:4-8** "Love is patient, love is kind. It does not envy; it does not boast; it is not proud. 5 It does not dishonor; it is not self-seeking; it is not easily angered; it keeps no record of wrongs. 6 Love does not delight in evil but rejoices with the truth. 7 It always protects, always trusts, always hopes, always perseveres. 8 Love never fails."

Mastering just one of these attributes can take a lifetime. Will you purpose in your heart to start today? I promise that it will be worth the effort as you both live in harmony. Please say this prayer:

"Father, I desire that you help my future spouse and me to master our love walk. Lord, please show us the areas that need improvement and help us as we do our part. We desire to Love you, each other, and your people as we do your will. Thank you, Lord. In Jesus' name, Amen."

Day 21
Meditate on Your Identity in Christ

As people who live in the world, we often see ourselves according to what we do. A mother, a father, Engineer, teacher, etc. It is usually when trials come that our identities are shaken. What if we are not able to teach, be a mother or Engineer anymore? Life happens, which is sometimes fraught with extremely adverse circumstances. It is during these times that we must remember that we are citizens of Heaven and children of the Most High God. We must not forget that our identity can never be shaken as we abide in Christ (John 15:4). When two people who are surrendered to God know who they are, they can bear much fruit for God and His Kingdom no matter their occupational or parental roles. Use the following as a prayer and give God thanks for each one.

Remember your identity in Christ

1. You are dearly loved **1 John 4:10**.
2. You were made in God's image, **Gen 1:26**.
3. You are chosen by God and are dearly loved, **Colossians 3:12**.
4. You are blameless and free from accusation, **Colossians 1:22**.
5. Christ is in you, **Colossians 1:27**.
6. God will always cause you to triumph in Christ Jesus, **2 Corinthians 2:14**.
7. The Lord watches over all of your ways, **Psalm 1:6**.
8. God's thoughts of you outnumber the sands of the Earth, **Psalm 139:17 & 18**.
9. You are anointed by God, **1 John 2:27**.
10. You are a member of a chosen, and a royal priesthood, a holy nation, **1 Peter 2:9-10**.

Day 22

Pray That You and Your Future Spouse Find Your Roles in The Body of Christ

As Christians, we all have our roles to play. After all, you both should be connected to a relevant, local ministry that is effective in serving God's people and the world. **1 Corinthians 12:27-31**, tells us the roles that we may be gifted for. It could be more than one. Are you currently involved in one of these roles? If you are not sure, God is ready to direct you to the area that you are best gifted in and most suited for. Trust Him in this area, and He will place you in the body where you will best serve the body of Christ. While there, don't forget that He is the vinedresser. As the branch, as you abide in the vine (Jesus), God will prune you as you produce fruit, even much more and excellent fruits. Pruning is no fun but necessary (John 15:5-8). Kindly say this prayer:

"Dear Heavenly Father, I desire to do your will, and I want to serve you in the place that you need me most. I pray the same for my future spouse. Lead and guide us, Lord. Help us to grow in you as we serve your people with a humble heart and contrite spirit. Help us to abide in the vine and give us courage and patience to endure the pruning process. May we serve with a spirit of excellence and be open to correction when needed. Thank you, Lord. I pray in Jesus' name, Amen."

Day 23
Worship While You Wait

Paul and Silas were doing God's work when they cast a foul spirit out of a woman. Her masters were using her to make money from the foul spirit. They became angry because Paul interrupted their income stream and had them arrested. Paul and Silas were laid on, beaten and thrown into prison. It is important to note that you could be doing the right thing for the right reasons and still be severely persecuted, so do not be surprised (Acts 16:16-36).

They were jailed and put in stocks. Instead of getting discouraged and depressed, they started praying and singing hymns to God. The other prisoners listened. Suddenly there was an earthquake that shook the foundations of the prison. The cells' doors were opened, and the shackles of all the prisoners came off. The jailer was going to harm himself because he thought they all escaped. Paul encouraged him that they were still all there. The jailer recognized what the power of God had done and wanted to know how he could be saved.

We have no idea what God is doing behind the scenes on our behalf. However, like Paul and Silas, if only we would turn our attention to God, pray and worship Him, the closed doors of the issues of our lives will open as well. say this prayer:

Dear Heavenly Father, I thank You that You hear when I pray (Psalm 100:4). I will bless You Lord and will continually offer You the sacrifice of praise (Psalm 34:1). Teach me to praise you as I patiently wait for your answer and resolve. In Jesus' name, Amen.

Day 24

Pray Against A Love for The World

We live in a world that loves to be showy. All too often, people like to show off what they have, what they're doing, what their eating, and how they are living on social media. They attribute success with positions, possessions and unique experiences. Having beautiful things and being around certain people makes them feel good about themselves. However, this is a trap. They are only showing you the good times and fun times. Once some or all of these things are lost or taken away, what may also go with it is their self-esteem. 1 John 2:15-17 (NKJV) addresses it this way: "Do not love the world or the things of the world. If anyone loves the world, the love of the Father is not in him. 16 For all that is in the world - the lust of the flesh, the lust of the eyes, and the pride of life - is not of the Father but is of the world. 17 And the world is passing away, and the lust of it; but he who does the will of God abides forever."

Please do not misunderstand. I am not saying there is anything wrong with having nice things or having wealth. We have to understand that God owns it all and that we are merely stewards of all that He gives.

We should remember that as a result of what our Lord did for us on the cross, we are now Ambassadors of Christ (2 Corinthians 5:20). We are also citizens of Heaven (Philippians 3:20). We are a chosen generation, royal priesthood belonging to a Holy nation (1 Peter 2:9). That said, nothing on this Earth can compare with our real home or identity. Kindly say this prayer:

"Dear Heavenly Father, thank you, Lord, for sending your only Son to die in my place. Help me always to remember the love He has shown for me. Therefore, anything in this world has to offer pales in comparison. As my future spouse and I keep our eyes on you, we thank you that you will strengthen us not to entangle ourselves with or love the things of this world. In Jesus' name, Amen."

Day 25

Pray That You and Your Future Spouse Make Righteousness A Priority

To be "righteous" simply means to be in "Right Standing" with God. Because of Jesus, God calls us the "righteousness of God through Christ" 2 Corinthians 5:21. This means that God sees us as already righteous in our spirit. However, He, by the power of the Holy Spirit will help us grow in our lives to be righteous people.

Living a righteous life not only brings eternal benefits but practical ones as well. Proverbs 11:6, 8 (NIV) says: "The righteousness of the upright delivers them, but the unfaithful are trapped by evil desires. 8 The righteous person is rescued from trouble, and it falls on the wicked instead.

The Bible declares that even the desires of the righteous benefit them. Proverbs 11:23 (NIV) says "The desire of the righteous ends only in good, but the hope of the wicked only in wrath." Living in a way that is in right standing with God has benefits on Earth! Proverbs 11:31 (NIV) "If the righteous receive their due on earth, how much more the ungodly and the sinner!" say this prayer:

"Father in Jesus' name and according to 2 Corinthians 5:21 (NIV), "God made him who had no sin to be sin for us; so that in Him we might become the righteousness of God." I thank you for the power of the Holy Spirit that will help me and my future spouse to walk in righteousness. We want all that you have for us, and we seek to be the servants you have called us to be, for you, Your glory and each other. I receive it now in Jesus' name, Amen.

Day 26

Pray That You Both Will Watch Your Speech

In the world, you are often judged first by how you look, then by how you speak. As Christians, we are not supposed to talk the way non-Christians do. In fact, God expects us to speak as He does. Proverbs 18:21 (NKJV) says: "Death and life are in the power of the tongue, And those who love it will eat its fruit." God speaks things that are not as though they were. Romans 4:17 says "As it is written, I have made thee a father of many nations, in the presence of Him whom he believed -God, who gives life to the dead and calls those things which do not exist as though they did." In other words, we can speak to things, situations and call them what we desire them to be, using the present tense.

We are also to encourage others in their faith 1 Thessalonians 3:2. That is the positive way we can use our speech. Psalm 52:1-3, Psalm 34:13 give us explicit instruction as to why we should avoid negative speech. Practice what you have studied in the aforementioned scriptures. Doing so will bring a tangible benefit to your future marriage and your life. Please say this prayer:

"Father, I am thankful for the wisdom in your word concerning the use of my words. May my future spouse and I learn and practice these principles. Bring your wisdom to our minds when we need it most, especially before we speak. Help us to continue to meditate and use what we learn. In Jesus' name, Amen.

Day 27

For Men: He Who Finds A Wife Finds A Good Thing

The day you marry the love of your life will likely be one of the most amazing events in your life. You will look into her beautiful face, and her eyes will sparkle as she returns your smile while standing before the altar. She will have a look of love and adoration for you. She will be placing her life, her everything into your care, confidently trusting you as you both enter the covenant, declaring your wedding vows before God and everyone that day.

As you grow together as "one," there will be challenges, hurt feelings, and disagreements. As life goes on, circumstances will challenge, even pummel your conviction to keep your vows to your lovely wife. When those days come, remember what God said in Proverbs 18:22 "He who finds a wife finds a good thing and obtains favor from the Lord."

To be completely clear, the definition of "Favor" is 1) Something done or granted out of goodwill, rather than from justice or for remuneration. 2) friendly or well-disposed regard 3) the state of being approved or held in regard 4) excessive kindness or unfair partiality; preferential treatment.

There is a special "favor" that God bestows on a man who gets married. It is likely because he will absolutely need it. There is no simulation for marriage. No one can fully prepare you for its nuances and unique interactions with your future wife. Be comforted because you are not in this by yourself. God will give you favor, and He is there to hear and answer your prayers. I highly recommend that you also read the best relationship books that you can find. In this way, you are not totally ignorant and unprepared. Knowing that you have access to supernatural help will make all the difference in making your marriage successful. Kindly say this prayer:

"Dear Heavenly Father, I look forward to receiving your favor bestowed upon me on my wedding day according to Proverbs 18:22. Help me to learn and prepare myself to be worthy of your favor and the bride you bring into my life. I ask you to continue to build good character in me as a man and a servant of Christ so I may be well prepared to love and serve her. I pray that I may never take her for granted nor frustrate the favor you will bestow upon me from my wedding day forward. Thank you, Lord, for hearing this prayer in Jesus' name, Amen.

Day 28

For Women: What Submission Really Means in The Context of Marriage and Why You Should Pray for The Ability to Do It

The word submission to women seems to be a dirty word in the United States and has been for a long time. This is likely due to 1) Ignorant men who witnessed an ignorant father who would mistreat their wives outside Biblical instructions to love them like Christ, to the point of humiliating and battering them in the home. 2) The word submission was methodically and deliberately taken out of context by the lies of the feminist movement, thus indoctrinating little girls to resist the idea of submission, who would then grow up to be women.

The definition of the word submission as it relates to the context of what Paul is saying is this: Submission 1) The action or fact of accepting or yielding to a superior force or the will or authority of another. 2) To give way to influence, entreaty, argument. 3) To give place or precedence.

Most of us have a driver's license and if not, kindly play along. Imagine that you are operating a midsize car that weighs about 4000 lbs. You have three passengers and are entering a three-lane, high-speed highway. You are in the acceleration lane, and the speed limit on this highway is 75 miles per hour. As you accelerate from 45 to 75 mph, the acceleration lane begins to merge with the highway traffic. As it does, a Heavy Equipment Transport tractor-trailer, carrying a Caterpillar D-9 bulldozer is approaching. Its combined weight is over 130,000 lbs.

The tractor-trailer is efficient in its purpose to move the bulldozer along the road and over long distances. It can also be devastatingly destructive to a 4000 lbs car that will get in its way, possibly causing mortal harm to you and your passengers. Your best decision would be to give it the "right of way" or "yield" to its path as you enter the highway. After all, the tractor-trailer driver is doing his job by operating safely. According to traffic laws, entering the highway safely is your responsibility.

Most everyone knows the scripture text of Ephesians 5:22-24 that says "Wives, submit yourselves to your husbands as you do to the Lord. 23 For the husband is the head of the wife as Christ is the head of the church, his body, of which he is the Savior. 24 Now, as the church submits to Christ, so also wives should submit to their husbands in everything."

Ladies, do not feel that you are alone in this because verse 21 also says: "Submit to one another out of reverence for Christ."

Colossians 3:18 has a different view of the same instruction. However, if we focus on verse 18 of the passage alone, we miss the whole context of what is being said. If you would start from verse 1, Paul discusses the need for a perspective that focuses on the bigger picture of the Christian life. Our Lord is Jesus, and our home is Heaven. That said, do not get tripped up on the small things on Earth. However, while you are here, the following should be your view and conduct. I like how the Amplified version talks about submission.

Col 3:18 (Amp) Wives, be subject to your husbands [out of respect for their position as protector, and their accountability to God], as is proper and fitting in the Lord.

Marriage, in essence, is a ministry as unto God. As you minister to your husband in the role of his wife, you are honoring God. Submission is not a request or suggestion, but a command. Your future husband will be accountable to God for his actions and is the head of your household, the Priest of your home. He should be the one who covers you with his daily prayers. He will be your lover and friend. But here is something I believe wives all too often forget. He is also your protector.

In other words, your husband will literally give his life to save you if your mortality was threatened. He would do so without thought or hesitation. He is created this way on purpose. He will willingly die in your place. Who else has already given their life in your place? Jesus. Kindly DO NOT take this lightly or for granted. If such an unfortunate event happened, of course, you would appreciate such a sacrifice with reverent gratitude and awe. Therefore, you should fully and soberly appreciate it daily while he's living.

With this perspective, ask yourself: "Is it so hard to give precedence or "yield" to your loving future husband? Is it so hard to do something he would ask you if it was Biblical, ethical, moral and lawful? The obvious answer should be no. Humbly say this prayer.

"Dear Heavenly Father, I come to you with a humble heart. I thank you in advance for a loving husband with a heart like Christ Jesus, my Lord, and Savior. Develop in me a will and determination to be submissive to my husband, as stated in scripture. I will serve you in all things Lord and give precedence to him as my lover and friend who would give his life to protect me. Thank you for your grace and such a wonderful gift of my husband. I pray in Jesus' name, Amen.

Day 29

Pray for A Heart That Submits to Christ

Ephesians 5 is famous for being the marriage chapter. Everyone knows what's coming as the verse starts with "Wives." However, just one verse before verse 22, there is verse 21 that says, "Submit to one another out of reverence for Christ." Indeed, both husbands and wives are to submit. In fact, because the husband is the head of the household, he should be the one that sets the example...first.

There is a saying in the military that "Leaders lead from the front." As I thoroughly covered submission for wives concerning their husbands in the previous segment, to be clear, no one is exempt. Ephesians 5:20 starts by saying that we should always give thanks to God for all things. Being thankful is the beginning of submission. When you realize that everything that you are, that you have, and everything that you can do is because of God's grace, or unmerited favor. You did not deserve it. You could not earn it. You had no right to all that God has done for you. He merely gave you the opportunities, the resources and the current life that you have based on HIS goodness, not ours.

The King of Kings and Lord of Lords submitted Himself to even death on a cross for our sake. Is it too much to submit ourselves to Him by submitting ourselves to each other? I close with this. Jesus could have called legions of Angels (One legion could be from 3000-6000 Angels) to come to His aid if He wanted to save himself from the cross. This same Jesus said, "Father, not my will, but yours be done." Luke 22:42.

Another example is when Jesus took off His robes, put on a towel like a slave and washed his disciple's feet. Imagine what marriages today would be like if husbands and wives lived a life of continual submission in their hearts towards each other like Jesus? I would say that there would no longer be a need for divorce attorneys or divorce courts. Kindly say this prayer:

"Dear Heavenly Father, I pray for a heart that entirely submits to you. Sometimes, my own will and emotions continuously get in the way of how I walk in accordance with your will and your way. Thank you in advance for the power of the Holy Spirit to help and guide me in all things. Help me to daily visualize, taking off my robes and putting on a towel to serve my spouse as you submitted yourself to your disciples and washed their feet. Fill me with Your Spirit that I may walk a victorious and submitted life in You today according to Ephesians 5:21. In Jesus' name, Amen.

Day 30

As a License Is to A Doctor to Practice Medicine,

Is Marriage to A Couple to Serve One Another

I write for online platforms, and I sometimes offer advice online on various topics, including marriage. I am often surprised by some of the questions. What seems to be at the core of many of these disturbing questions is selfishness. People want to draw their line in the sand or stake their claim concerning one notion or another within their own relationship. For example: If my husband doesn't do this for me, I'm going to do that...or I want to do this, but she doesn't want to do what I want, etc.

The Apostle Paul states in Ephesians 5:17 (NIV) "Therefore, do not be foolish but understand what the Lord's will is." He continues in verse 21 "Submit to one another out of reverence for Christ." I have fully explained in previous segments what the true concept of submission is. Again, in the context of this passage, it is an emotional, spiritual and physical posture of yielding to your spouse. Ryan And Selena Frederick of the seven day "Fierce Marriage" devotional series, puts it this way: "You first."

One of the reasons why marriage sometimes doesn't work for secular couples is because they may be quite happy to marry before a priest or minister in the church, as a matter of tradition. But the reality is, they're coming together in covenant and saying their vows before a holy God with all present. They are saying "You first." Many years later, they may have forgotten their own words. They do not maintain this perspective, and it fades years later.

In the book of John 13:1-17 (NIV), Jesus displays His posture as a servant to his disciples. In verses 15-17 he says this: "15 I have set you an example that you should do as I have done for you. 16 Very truly I tell you, no servant is greater than his master, nor is a messenger greater than the one who sent him. 17 Now that you know these things, you will be blessed if you do them." Living a life as a servant of Christ is not an option. In fact, serving is our life. How much more to our spouse to whom we are in covenant with?

I recommend, on the night before your wedding day, that you both read over your wedding vows before bed. On your wedding anniversary, you and your spouse should read them to each other after that. May I suggest that daily, from morning to night, effort the posture of: "You first" Please say this prayer:

Dear Heavenly Father, give my future spouse and I the heart of a servant that walks in obedience to you before and after our marriage. Teach us to be followers of Jesus, and to yield and submit to one another with a servant's heart. Never let us take each other for granted or to become tired in well doing according to Galatians 6:9 & 10. May our relationship perpetually represent the love of Christ for His Bride; the church. In Jesus' name, Amen.

Day 31

Don't Forget to Have Fun

While you are praying for your future spouse, or perhaps you have already found someone. Whatever your situation, you must remember that life is God's gift and meant to be lived.

The book of Ecclesiastes 3:4 declares "A time to weep, and a time to laugh; a time to mourn, and a time to dance." When was the last time that you had a good "belly" laugh? When was the last time you danced? Perhaps you don't know-how. How about taking dance lessons? We serve a God who understands what it means to celebrate and be celebrated.

Don't let life pass you by as you are waiting for God's answer and provision. Do something for yourself, something you enjoy. Spend time with friends, call someone that you haven't spoken to in a while and tell them you thought of them and appreciate their friendship.

Having fun and enjoying the life God has given you gives Him pleasure. It says that you appreciate His wonderful gift of life. So, as the last day and segment of the book, there won't be a prayer suggested this time. Instead, go and have some fun!

Author's Last Words

Thank you for reading my book. It is my honor and pleasure to write informative books for my readers. I trust that you found this book helpful and that it was a blessing to you. If you feel that it was, would you kindly show your appreciation and write a review on Amazon, Goodreads or Google Books? I would greatly appreciate your assistance to help to get the word out.

Thank you again, and I pray for your outstanding success in your marriage!

-John Williams

Author Contact

Amazon Author Page
https://www.amazon.com/John-Williams/e/B00BUPWR64

Email Address:
john.williams.author@gmail.com

Twitter
https://twitter.com/JWilliams_Auth

Facebook
https://www.facebook.com/JWilliamsflask

Quora
https://www.quora.com/profile/John-Williams-1222

Made in the USA
Columbia, SC
26 February 2021